P9-ECL-291

A Primary Source Guide to

PAKISTAN

Kerri O'Donnell

The Rosen Publishing Group's

PowerKids Press™

PRIMARY SOURCE

New York

Published in 2003 by The Rosen Publishing Group, Inc.
29 East 21st Street, New York, NY 10010

Book Design: Haley Wilson

Photo Credits: Cover, p. 1 © The Image Bank; p. 4 © Map Resources; pp. 6, 8 (inset), 19 © Corbis; pp. 6 (inset), 12 © Roger Wood/Corbis; p. 8 by J. B. Wilkinson; p. 10 © AFP/Corbis; p. 14 © Galen Rowell/Corbis; p. 16 © Ed Kashi/Corbis; p. 16 (inset) © Earl & Nazima Kowall/Corbis; p. 18 © Arthur Thevenart/Corbis; p. 20 © Jonathan Blair/Corbis; p. 22 © Eyewire.

Library of Congress Cataloging-in-Publication Data

O'Donnell, Kerri, 1972-
  A primary source guide to Pakistan / Kerri O'Donnell.
      p. cm. — (The Rosen Publishing Group's PowerKids Press)
Summary: Describes the geography, people, history, economy, and culture of Pakistan.
  ISBN: 0-8239-6595-3 (library binding)
  ISBN: 0-8239-8079-0 (pbk.)
  6-pack ISBN: 0-8239-8086-3
  1. Pakistan—Juvenile literature. [1. Pakistan.] I. Title. II. Series.
  DS376.9 .O36 2003
  954.91—dc21
                          2002004900

Manufactured in the United States of America

Contents

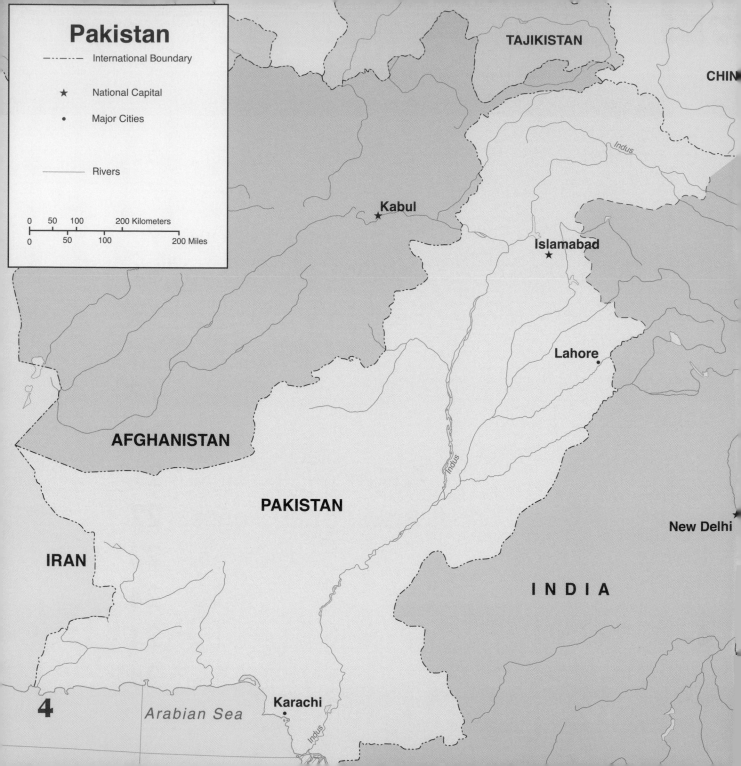

Pakistan

- **-··-··-** International Boundary
- ★ National Capital
- • Major Cities
- —— Rivers

0 50 100   200 Kilometers
0 50   100   200 Miles

TAJIKISTAN

CHIN

Kabul ★

Islamabad ★

Lahore •

AFGHANISTAN

PAKISTAN

New Delhi ★

IRAN

I N D I A

Indus

Indus

4 Arabian Sea

Karachi •

Indus

Pakistan

Pakistan is a country in southern Asia. Several countries border Pakistan, including Afghanistan to the northwest and India to the east. Almost all of Pakistan's people are **Muslim**, which means they practice a religion called **Islam**. Religion is very important to the people of Pakistan. It is the main reason that Pakistan became an independent nation in the mid-1900s.

Today, Pakistan is a troubled country. Pakistan is often at war with its neighbor, India, because of the differences between their beliefs.

◀ In 2001, the United States went to war with a group of people, many of whom lived in Afghanistan. Pakistan's government has given the United States a lot of help in this war.

6

Very few people live in western Pakistan because it is very dry and not much can grow there. Most people live in Pakistan's northeastern plains where the soil is better for growing crops. This area is called the Punjab. In the Punjabi language, "*punjab*" means "five rivers." Pakistan's capital, Islamabad, is in the Punjab. Pakistan also has high, snow-covered mountains. The world's second-highest mountain, called K2, is located in northern Pakistan.

Pakistan gets an average of only about ten inches of rain a year! Most of the rain falls in the summer, when strong winds blow across the land.

◄ Different parts of Pakistan get different amounts of rain. The southwestern desert area, shown in the small photo, gets fewer than five inches a year. The eastern Punjab gets more than twenty inches of rain a year. The large photo shows Attock Fort on the Indus River in the northern Punjab.

An Act to make provision for the setting up in India of two independent Dominions, to substitute other provisions for certain provisions of the Government of India Act, 1935, which apply outside those Dominions, and to provide for other matters consequential on or connected with the setting up of those Dominions.

[18th July 1947.]

BE it enacted by the King's most Excellent Majesty, by and with the advice and consent of the Lords Spiritual and Temporal, and Commons, in this present Parliament assembled, and by the authority of the same, as follows :—

1.—(1) As from the fifteenth day of August, nineteen hundred and forty-seven, two independent Dominions shall be set up in India, to be known respectively as India and Pakistan.

(2) The said Dominions are hereafter in this Act referred to as " the new Dominions ", and the said fifteenth day of August is hereafter in this Act referred to as " the appointed day ".

2.—(1) Subject to the provisions of subsections (3) and (4) of this section, the territories of India shall be the territories under the sovereignty of His Majesty which, immediately before the appointed day, were included in British India except the territories which, under subsection (2) of this section, are to be the territories of Pakistan.

Territories of the new Dominions.

(2) Subject to the provisions of subsections (3) and (4) of this section, the territories of Pakistan shall be—

(a) the territories which, on the appointed day, are included in the Provinces of East Bengal and West Punjab,

Pakistan's history started more than 4,500 years ago when a **civilization** developed around the Indus River. The civilization lasted for about 800 years.

For the next few thousand years, people from different lands settled in the area. In the 1800s and early 1900s, the British controlled the area, and it was known as "British India." India won its freedom from Britain in 1947 and the land was divided into two parts based on religion. Northwestern and northeastern India had many Muslims and became East Pakistan and West Pakistan, which were separated by 1,000 miles of Indian land.

◀ The statue shown here is from the Indus River valley civilization and is at least 3,500 years old! The document is the Indian Independence Act written by British Parliament in 1947. It stated that British India would be split into two independent countries: India and Pakistan.

10

Pakistan's Politics

In 1948, Pakistan and India went to war over Kashmir, an area of land they both claimed. The two countries continue to fight over this land today. In 1971, a **civil war** broke out between East Pakistan and West Pakistan. East Pakistan became an independent nation called Bangladesh.

In 1973, Pakistan adopted a new **constitution**. In 1999, a general named Pervez Musharraf took control of the country and **suspended** the constitution. He told the Pakistani people that he did this to find "another path to **democracy**." Musharraf believed the previous leaders were dishonest.

◀ After taking over the leadership of Pakistan, Musharraf reassured the people that he wanted to improve their way of life. "In the past," he said, "our governments have ruled the people. It is now time for the government to serve the people."

Pictured here is the 100-rupee banknote. The man pictured on the banknote is Muhammad Ali Jinnah who is known as the founder of Pakistan.

Farming in Pakistan

Pakistan's economy depends mainly on farming. Most people make their living by growing crops or raising animals. Pakistan's largest crop is wheat, but cotton, rice, sugarcane, fruits, and vegetables are also grown there. Many farmers raise goats, sheep, and cattle for their milk, meat, and hides. Fishing is also an important business in Pakistan.

Pakistan also produces clothing, flour, sugar, leather goods, and rugs. These goods are traded for things the country needs, like iron, steel, machinery, and food products.

◀ Many people in Pakistan are craftworkers. They make things like rugs, pottery, and clothing that they sometimes sell in markets like this one.

The People of Pakistan

The government, large companies, and universities in Pakistan have access to modern **technology**, but most of Pakistan's people do not. The people who live in Pakistan's small villages are farmers, and they are usually very poor. Many people live in two-room houses made of clay or mud with dirt floors. Pakistan's cities have modern brick houses in crowded neighborhoods. People who live in the cities often work in shops and factories, but they make little money.

◀ Pakistani men have much more freedom than women. Most women don't work outside the home, although some help with the farming. In many of the small villages, women and girls must wear traditional Muslim head coverings called *chadurs* when they leave their homes.

Islam

Ninety-seven percent of Pakistan's people practice Islam, the religion preached by the **prophet** Muhammad about 1,400 years ago. Muhammad believed that he had been sent to teach people about God, or Allah. The **Qur'an** is a holy book that Muslims believe Allah sent to them through Muhammad.

Muslims pray five times a day. On Fridays, they go to a **mosque** to pray. They say words from the Qur'an, kneel, and bow toward Mecca, the city in Saudi Arabia where Muhammad was born.

◀ The Badshahi Mosque is located in Lahore, Pakistan, and was built by Emperor Aurangzeb in 1674. About 10,000 Muslins can pray in the courtyard of this mosque at one time. The small image is a copy of the Qur'an that is about 1,200 years old.

Much of Pakistan's art is based on the Islamic religion. Mosques and other religious buildings are often decorated with colorful tiles arranged in

beautiful patterns. Pakistanis also make brightly patterned cloth, pottery, rugs, and objects made of wood, glass, and ivory. The most popular music in Pakistan is Qawwali, which is performed by a group of men singing, clapping, and playing drums.

This tomb is decorated with thousands of brightly colored tiles. Many buildings also feature artistic handwriting called calligraphy. The calligraphy shown here is written in Arabic, which is a common language in southern Asia. It is read from right to left.

19

An Uncertain Future

People in Pakistan have many differences. There are four regions in Pakistan, and each has its own language. Many of Pakistan's people are poor and lead difficult lives. Because there aren't enough schools, many people don't know how to read or write. Some, however, are very successful. Dr. Abdus Salam, a Pakistani scientist, won a **Nobel prize** in 1979.

Pakistan's problems with India over land and differing beliefs have led to fighting. Maybe someday soon there will be peace in Pakistan.

◀ Schools in Pakistan are usually small. Some children go to school in the morning and some go in the evening so the schools are not too crowded.

Pakistan at a Glance

Population: About 145,000,000

Capital City: Islamabad (population about 530,000)

Largest City: Karachi (population about 14 million)

Official Name: The Islamic Republic of Pakistan

National Anthem: "Qaumi Tarana" ("National Anthem")

Land Area: 307,374 square miles (796,095 square kilometers)

Government: Republic

Unit of Money: Pakistani rupee

Flag: The star and crescent moon on Pakistan's flag are the symbols of Islam.

Glossary

civilization (sih-vuh-luh-ZAY-shun) A way of life followed by the people of a certain time and place.

civil war (SIH-vuhl WOHR) A war between different groups of people living in the same country.

constitution (kahn-stuh-TOO-shun) The basic rules of a country or state.

democracy (dih-MAH-kruh-see) A government run by the people.

Islam (is-LAHM) A religion based on the teachings of a prophet named Muhammad that appear in the Qur'an.

mosque (MAHSK) A building where Muslims go to pray.

Muslim (MUHZ-luhm) A person who practices Islam.

Nobel prize (noh-BELL PRYZE) Annual prizes given to people who work for the good of everyone.

prophet (PRAH-fuht) A religious leader who claims to speak as directed by God.

Qur'an (kuh-RAN) The holy book of the Islamic religion.

suspend (suh-SPEND) To stop something temporarily.

technology (tek-NAH-luh-jee) The use of science to solve a problem.

23

Index

Primary Source List

Page 6. Attock Fort, on the Indus River, Punjab. Completed in 1583 under the supervision of Khawaja Shamsuddin Khawafi, one of the emperor Akbar's ministers.

Page 8. Part of the Indian Independence Act, 1947. The original is in the Public Record Office of Britain's National Archives.

Page 8 (inset). Priest-King. From ruins of the Indus River valley city of Mohenjadaro, at least 3,500 years old. Now in the National Museum in Karachi.

Page 10. Photograph of Pervez Musharraf being sworn in as president. Taken by a Reuters news photographer, June 20, 2001.

Page 12 (inset). One-hundred-rupee banknote, with portrait of Muhammad Ali Jinnah.

Page 14. Girl wearing traditional Muslim head covering. Photograph taken in Chongo Village in Braldu Valley, ca. 1989.

Page 16. Badshahi Mosque in Lahore. Built during the reign of Aurangzeb Alamgir, 1658–1707.

Page 16 (inset). Qur'an, ca. 800 A.D. Now in Srinagar, Kashmir.

Page 18. Tomb of Sultan Ali Akbar, who died in 1605. In Multan.

Page 19. Passage from the Hadith on wall of Wazir Khan Mosque. Built by Hakim Ilmud Din Ansari, who was given title of Wazir Khan (or chief minister) by Shah Jahan. Built 1634–1641. In Lahore.

Page 20. Boys reading from textbooks. Photograph taken in September 1991. At Aga Khan Diamond Jubilee School in village of Chumar Khan.

Web Sites

Due to the changing nature of Internet links, The Rosen Publishing Group, Inc. has developed an on-line list of Web sites related to the subjects of this book. This site is updated regularly. Please use this link to access the list:
http://www.powerkidslinks.com/pswc/pspa/